Valentine Poetry

Love Poems for the Everyday Lovers

r. A. bentinck

FYAPUBLISHING | GEORGETOWN

Copyright © 2021 by **r. A. bentinck**

All rights reserved. No part t of this book may be reproduced or utilized in any form or by any means, electronically or mechanically, including photocopying, recording, or by any information storage or retrieval system, without permission in writing from the Author or Publisher. Inquiries should be addressed to FyaPublishing.

**FyaPublishing
95 South Turkeyen,
Georgetown, Guyana.**

Valentine Poetry r. A. bentinck
ISBN 978-0999444580

Cover design by **Rebecacovers**

For the everyday lovers

"Two hearts in love need no words"

— *MARCELINE DESBORDES-VALMORE*
French Poet

Contents

Chapter One: Young Love _____ 17

    Please, Cupid _____ *19*

    Love Calls _____ *20*

    Our First Time _____ *21*

    Innocence _____ *23*

    On My Mind _____ *24*

    In My Head _____ *25*

    I Hope _____ *26*

    Use to Be _____ *27*

    Your Ways _____ *28*

    The List _____ *29*

    Exposed _____ *30*

    A Different Smile _____ *31*

    Naive _____ *32*

    Living In The Moment _____ *33*

Chapter Two: Breathing Love _____ 35

    Chocolate, Please _____ *37*

    Dining On The Floor _____ *39*

    Binge Watching _____ *40*

    Hansel And Gretel _____ *41*

Picking Flowers	*43*
Flirt With Me	*44*
Morning Glow	*46*
Slow Dance	*47*
Morning Coffee	*48*
Illuminated Memories	*49*
In the Park	*50*
Unspeakable	*51*
A Blanket Of Petals	*52*
Don't Speak	*53*
Chapter Three: You Own My Heart	*55*
A Blanket	*57*
Waking Up	*58*
Wine Glasses	*59*
Smartphones	*60*
Reading a Classic	*61*
Her Voice	*63*
Intuition	*64*
Smile	*65*
February 14th	*66*
If I Could	*67*

Her Eyes	68
For Everything	69
The Smile	70
This Morning	71

Chapter Four: Hardcore Loving — 73

Forgiven	75
From the Valleys of Love	76
Ghetto Love	78
Loving the Hurt Away	79
These Streets (Raggamuffin Love)	81
Forbidden Love	82
Dangerous	83
One Night Dilemma	84
Locked Up	85
The Meaning of Love	86
Uncertainty	87
Ride or Die Love	88
Uncompromising	89
Gangster Loving	90

Chapter Five: Teen Love — 91

Finally	93

She Is	94
Criminals	95
Fear	96
Fell	97
Foolish Heart	98
In My Dreams	99
Lion King	100
Perception	101
Puppy Love	102
Rebel	103
Smitten	104
Unexpected	105
Pixie Dust	106
Chapter Six: You Are The Reason	107
Fall Asleep	109
Matching	110
Illuminated	111
Heaven Knows	112
Ever-Present	113
Blowing Kisses	114
No Rules	115

Your Kisses	*116*
Distance Lovers	*117*
The Patient Lover	*118*
One Day	*119*
Notifications	*120*
Perfection	*121*
Goodbyes	*122*
Chapter Seven: Falling For You	*123*
Animality	*125*
Rainy Thoughts	*126*
My Favourite Things	*127*
The Scent of a Woman	*128*
Legality	*129*
Unfriendly	*131*
Connecting Conversations	*133*
Window Curtains	*134*
Word Search	*135*
Slow	*136*
3 A.M.	*137*
Slow Kisses	*138*
Dress to Kill	*139*

Sun Kissed _____ *140*

Chapter Eight: The Look Of Love _____ *141*

Heartbeat _____ *141*

Thoughts _____ *144*

Heated Smile _____ *145*

Always _____ *146*

Rainy Rhythms _____ *148*

Relaxation (food for the soul) _____ *149*

The Model Student _____ *150*

I Will Wait _____ *151*

Lullabies _____ *152*

Teach Me _____ *153*

The Stars _____ *155*

Thoughts of You _____ *156*

Inexplicable _____ *157*

Changes _____ *158*

Chapter Nine: Mellow Moods _____ *159*

Mornings Of Memories _____ *161*

Complicated _____ *162*

Heartbeat _____ *163*

Chocolate Lollipops _____ *164*

You Are	165
Kiss Me Again	166
Without Saying A Word	168
Top Down	169
Your Memories	170
Rekindled	171
Time Watcher	172
Love From A Distance	174
Sweet Talk You	177
Innocently	178

Chapter Ten: A Love Supreme — 179

The Sweetness From Your Lips	181
Desirable	182
In Your Eyes	183
Pee	184
Late Night Dinner	185
I Wish	186
In My Mind	187
She Said...	188
Tired Feet	189
Oxygen	190

One More Time	191
Steppin' Out	192
Raindrops	193
Heading Home	195

Chapter Eleven: Overjoyed — 197

Take Me There Again	199
Every-Day-Love	200
Morning Glory	201
Sunrise	202
Love's Crescendo Afterglow	204
Daybreak	206
Her Kisses	207
I Want To Hold You	208
Caribbean Spice	209
Just One Thought	210
Morning Wish	211
Flaming Desires	212
The Little Things	213
Never Forget	214

Chapter Twelve: Being With You — 215

Cuddling	217

Touch	218
I See You	219
Pillow Talk	220
A Message a Day	221
Half-Past Crazy	222
You	223
Pillows And Sheets	224
Because	225
Another You	226
No More Fairytales	227
No Competition	228
Electricity	229
35,000 Feet Up High-Cruising Altitude	230

Chapter Thirteen: Love Test — 231

Choices	233
Bedtime Stories	234
Complicated	235
Giving Up	236
I Thought About It	237
It's Not Perfect	238
Never Alone	239

Temptation's Valleys ———————— 240

Preserve The Garden ———————— 241

Happily Ever After ———————— 242

Picking Up The Pieces ———————— 243

Fear ———————— 244

Termites To Love ———————— 245

Contemplation ———————— 246

Chapter Fourteen: Lasting Love ———————— 247

Why ———————— 249

Learners ———————— 250

Adjustments ———————— 251

Daily Deposits ———————— 252

Daily Habits ———————— 253

Damn! ———————— 254

Longevity ———————— 255

Mastery ———————— 256

No Retreat, No Surrender ———————— 257

Revenge ———————— 258

Story Time ———————— 259

Time, Love And Tenderness ———————— 260

Without a Word ———————— 261

The Little Things _____ *262*

About The Author _____ *263*

Chapter One: Young Love

r. A. bentinck

Please, Cupid

there is so much
about this love
that feels so right,
what do we need
to do to make this last
forever?

**cupid, please show us
your secret formula.**

let's do the things
that makes this love
last longer and
grow stronger,

let the roots
that nourish this love
go deeper.

**cupid, please fertilizer
our love.**

we don't just want
our hearts to merge
but our body and soul.

**cupid, please heed
our pleas,**

show us the way
to make this love last
for always.

r. A. bentinck

Love Calls

you winked
at me
and i smiled
in acknowledgement.

in that brief
and **innocuous gesture**
we found
the clues to our
mutual feelings.

we passed by each other
eyes fixated and
a permanent smile
highlighted our faces,

**we didn't know it then
but we do now.**

it was **the call of love**
and **we answered.** ♥

Our First Time

i remember
the first time
my uncertain hands
slothfully traced
the contours of
your curvaceous hips.

i remember
holding you
so close i could feel
the heat in **every breath**
you took.

i remember
looking into
your eyes
and i saw your struggles
to bridle
your wild innocence.

i remember
you biting your begging lips
just to **conceal your hunger**
for what we both
was feeling.

i remember
your eyes shyly
falling to your feet,
i can still feel the softness
of **your cheeks** as i
picked your face up
reassuringly.

r. A. bentinck

i remember
how we **slowly gravitated**
to each other's magnetic lips.

i remember
the taste
and feel of
your baby kisses. ♥

Innocence

holding your hands
for the first time
releases butterflies
in my **mind,**

being close to your smile
electrify
the joys in my heart,

sharing your laughter
is the type of sound
i never will never
grow tired of hearing,

but it is kissing you
for the first time
that does things
to the cells in my body
that make them
fizz with delight. 🩶

r. A. bentinck

On My Mind

i cannot explain why
but
there is a certain
sweetness
that waters my mouth
every time i think
about you.

i search in vain
for words to describe
the tranquillity
that embraces me
every time thoughts
of you
dominates my mind. ♥

In My Head

you are like
that ideal love song,
you are always
in **my head**
even when it's not playing.

you marinate
my being to the extent
that you flavour
every meat on **my bones.**

you often paint
the colours that
enliven my face
every time your memories
surface. 🖤

r. A. bentinck

I Hope

i hope we never find
the words **to truly
describe how we**
feel about each other.

i hope we never get
tired of searching
for the reasons
that makes us
glossy-eyed
whenever we are in
each other's company.

i hope we continue
to ignore the **norms
and traditions**
of an oppressive society
regarding **our love;**

and **i hope we continue**
to appreciate and celebrate
**the uniqueness we share.
i hope this love continues**
to be a mystery
and **we never grow tired**
of searching for clues
to **get closer together.**

may we **forever
thirst** for
this undefined love. ♥

Use to Be

a kiss used to be
just **a kiss**
until i kissed you.

a smile used to be
just **a smile**
until you smiled at me.

a hug used to be
just **a hug**
until you hugged me.

"i love you" used to be
just **another expression**
until i heard it from you.

i used to dream a dream
i thought **wasn't possible**
in reality, and then
i met you. ♥

r. A. bentinck

Your Ways

you have a way
of **igniting** all
my senses
with the things you do
and the **subtle words**
you say.

you put me in
an anticipatory spin
that have me yearning
to be in your presence.

you already have
my attention
now
you are influencing
my love language.
you have **stripped me**
of my machoness
momentarily
and i don't intend to resist
the **things you intend**
to do to me. ♥

Valentine Poetry

The List

today
i am making a list.

i want to list
all the things
i cherish about you.

i want to
make a list
of all the things
i adore in you.

i want to count
the blessings
you have added
to my life.

today
i am making a list
because you have
been **so many**
things to me
in so many ways.

r. A. bentinck

Exposed

if she only knew
that **behind**
my bulb-like smile
and confident posture
was a mind filled
ideas like dried leaves
in a gale wind.

she opened the window
and exposed
my most private thoughts
to the **testy wind.**

now i am here
contemplating
whether my fantasies
can match up
with her realty. ♥

A Different Smile

mama looked at me
and **said adorable,**
*"i see you found love,
who is she?"*

**with a coy tone,
i responded,**
"who told you?"

"no one"
she replied smiling…
she continued,
*"these days you smile
with your entire face
instead of just your lips"*

i didn't realise
the extent of her impact
in my life,
mama said,
"She changed your smile,"
Wow! ♥

r. A. bentinck

Naive

after a year together
am i too naive
to be thinking
that maybe
you are the one that
stays for a lifetime?

am i seeing through
coloured lens
when i think,
you look like the
rest of my life
kind of lover?

did i fall this hard
for you
that i am losing my
logical sense of reasoning?
or is this
just your fairytale effect
seeping through me? ♥

Living In The Moment

you and me forever?

let's be honest,
we don't know.

what i do know
is that i will
love you every day
like it's the last day
i will get to love you.

i intend to create
lasting memories
that even if we
are not together
in the future
i will have enough
sweet memories of you
to sustain me
for as long as i yearn
for love.

i don't know what
our tomorrow will bring
but i will make today
count
in a significant way. 🩶

r. A. bentinck

Valentine Poetry

Chapter Two: Breathing Love

r. A. bentinck

Valentine Poetry

Chocolate, Please

lay it on me,
glacially,
please.

**the deep
dark
rich
creamy
goodness.**

chocolate, please,

no
not the kind
you find
in
the candy stores,
but
**the sweet
sugar words**
that flow
in abundance
from your mouth
to
the depths
of my being.

chocolate, please.
no, not
**Hershey's,
Ferrero Rocher,
Cadbury,**
or

r. A. bentinck

Godiva,
but
your syrupy touch
in
my craving places.

chocolate, please.

take me
to **chocolate heaven**
with **your milky ways.**

let me experience
each
complex flavours
found
in each morsel.
help me redefine
my taste experiences,
while developing
my connoisseurship

moment
by
moment.
chocolate, please. ♥

Valentine Poetry

Dining On The Floor

skimpily clad,
scented candles,
petals placed
strategically,

and the best of Sade
softly dominating
the background.

**our burgeoning
desires**
took possession
of the room.
finger foods
to complement
**the hidden gems
of the moment.**

tonight,
we do it differently
tonight,
we do it
creatively
**in every imaginable
way.
let's take-off**
inhibitions
and
toss them aside,
let's sync
with smoothness
and **savour each
surprising moment.** ♥

r. A. bentinck

Binge Watching

let's lined them up
our favourite
romantic movies
and **binge-watch**
the day away.

cue up **'Brown Sugar'**
and let Sidney and Dre
show us distance
doesn't dull the edge
of genuine love.

slip-on **'Love Jones'**
and let Darius and Nina
remind us of the power
of instant connection.

let's practice
our dance moves
like Johnny and Frances
in **'Dirty Dancing.'**

Monica and Quincy
will remind us
that love can blossom
while we have fun
playing
in **'Love and Basketball'**,
we can end the day with
'When Harry Met Sally"
or an all-time classic:
'Casablanca'
or **we can go on** and on. ♥

Hansel And Gretel

love notes
placed strategically
on the polished floor
to **welcome her**
home.

after a hard day's
work,
i intend to
pamper her

i will soothe her
tired feet
and
ease her
stressed mind.
i clean
the house,
washed
the dishes,
took care
of the bathroom
and
prepared and layout
the dining table.
then i set
my rescue plan
in motion.
i designed each note
to **destress**
and
declutter
her mind,

r. A. bentinck

each footstep
must increase
her anticipation.
each note scripted
to lead her to
the pleasure palace,

there
she will
unwind and loosen up. ♥

Valentine Poetry

Picking Flowers

i saw these on my way home
and i couldn't resist them.

**the fragrance
tickled my nose**
from kilometers away
and like a hound dog
i sniffed my way
to the concealed tree
laden
with these beauties.

i had to stop.
i had to **pick
these flowers**
because **they reminded me
so much of you.**

colours
that **engaged me,**
scent
that **enticed me,**
and
**silky to the touch.
i picked flowers today**
because
they reminded me
of you
in **unnumbered ways.** ♥

r. A. bentinck

Flirt With Me

break down
my false defences
with words
that **strip me** of
my inhibitions.

flirt with me.

let your **words**
fondle
my senses
rendering me
weak
to the touch
just waiting
to explode
in your presence.

flirt with me.
take me
to **that number cloud**
with
your skilled combination
of luscious words;
leaving me **gasping**
in anticipation.

flirt with me.

go to
your special dictionary
and plagiarise
sensual and

Valentine Poetry

flirtatious words
lay them
on me, please.
baby,
just **flirt with me,**
please. 🤍

r. A. bentinck

Morning Glow

she is like
my **morning rose,**

she adds
light,
fresh fragrance
and
bloom
to my days. ♥

Valentine Poetry

Slow Dance

we melt into
the **bosom**
of the music
while
our obedient feet
synced to each
rhythmic beat.

the songwriters seem
to know us
intimately.
every word mirrors
our current feelings
perfectly,
and
each **selection stimulated**
the ideal emotional cord.

with
eyes closed
and **emotions**
wide awake,
slow jams orchestrated
the moment's beauty.
dancing in the moonlight
amidst the whispers
of the night.
i won't consider
trading this moment
for millions. 🖤

r. A. bentinck

Morning Coffee

naw,
we are **not watching
the news**
this morning.

today,
it's coffee and
conversation.

we will share our
dreams and wishes
our doubts and fears.
this morning
will be
all about us.
let's sit on
the porch
and
greet the sun,
let's **cuddle**
because
the morning breeze
instruct us
to do so.
today,
let's enjoy
morning coffee
and conversation. ♥

Illuminated Memories

stringed lights
and **picture memories.**

let's create
a lighted wall of
our treasured memories.

let's hang
highlights of
our **photographed memories**
on the bedroom wall.

let's bring
light and life
to this room,
just me and you. ♥

r. A. bentinck

In the Park

a symphony of chirping birds,
and the sweet
accompanying melodies
of bees,

it's all i wish to hear
while relaxing
to **your heartbeat.**

let's
sit under
the **shaded tree**
while the sun
wend its way
to rest
in the west.
let's **lay** on
the grass bed
while we gaze
at the clouds,
and
count the creatures
we can trace
with **our imagination.**
let's release
the child inside
and **frolic bare feet**
in those old
carefree ways. ♥

Valentine Poetry

Unspeakable

take her
to **forbidden places**
often,
where

she yearns
to return

but is too timid
to talk about.

steal her breath
intermittently
with your
seductive creativity. ♥

r. A. bentinck

A Blanket Of Petals

let's ditch
the **familiar sheet**
let me lay you on
a **cotton cloud bed**
and
cover you with **petals.**

light our favourite
scented candle
and
let's surrender
to what
comes **naturally.**
fling inhibitions
outside the door,
and
invite adventure,

let me lay you down
on a blanket of petals
and
drive you insane
with rose petal
touches. ♥

Don't Speak

your hands
entwined **in mine.**

your hands
become
my hands.

shhhhh…
don't speak.
your eyes greet mine,
let eyes speak.

shhhh…
don't say a word.
let **the emotions**
flow-through
contracting veins
as we meekly
surrender in silence.

shhhh…
don't speak.
sometimes,
silence is the best elixir
for **a moment's thirst.**

r. A. bentinck

Valentine Poetry

Chapter Three: You Own My Heart

r. A. bentinck

A Blanket

a blanket for you
just because
i know
i cannot
always be there.

when the nights get
chilly
here is **a blanket**
with **a custom message**
just to keep you
warm.

a blanket for you
to **snuggle under**
whenever you
think of me. ♥

r. A. bentinck

Waking Up

i wanna wake up
to your arms
reaching over for me
while **you snuggle**
closer in **a warm embrace**
that **brings a gentle smile**
to **my face.**

i wanna awake
to the warmth
of your breathing
kissing me
intermittently,
on the shoulder.
i wanna **open my eyes**
to the renewed
confidence
of your daily love.

i wanna **rollover**
into the arms
of your love
that adds
fertilizer
to my daily bloom.

i'm in love
with waking up
to the feels,
the sights,
and the sounds
of being in bed
next to you. ♥

Valentine Poetry

Wine Glasses

crystal seducers
and **tea lights**
illuminated
the path.

half-filled glasses
of vintage wine
created **a scented**
trail.

to
a
bed adorned
with petals.
a virgin night
waiting on us
to take its **virginity.**

anticipation sends
butterflies
to decorate our insides.

eyes meet
and
instantly our
resistance faded
like a wuss. 🩶

r. A. bentinck

Smartphones

let's transform
our smartphones into
our bedroom.

you over there
and i'm over here.

serenade me with
your **texting slangs.**

make me weak
with your
suggestive emojis.

let's transform
our smartphones
into **seductive toys.**

play with
my emotions.

send me messages
that **colour**
my imagination,
heighten
my **anticipation**
and
salivate my desires. ♥

Reading a Classic

making love to you
should be like
reading
an excellent book.

your cover should be
examined in its entirety
each image noted
and **appreciated.**

you must be
turned over
with bated breath
and your blurb read
to enjoy the **synopsis**
of the goodness
to uncover.

you should be
opened with care
and each page
turned and digested.

every punctuation mark,
and **every page flip**
must be an experience
in **savouring quality.**

and when the end arrives
this book
should not be closed
abruptly,
but there must be

r. A. bentinck

a reflection
on the journey
just experienced.
then
**after a moment's
pause,**

i would return
to my favourite pages
and **reread them,**

slowly
indulging in
the **unending beauty**
and the experiences they offer
**again and again.
just like the classics**
you should be
reread
to savour each
delectable
and **breathtaking moment**

with the intension
of catching any
nuances missed
because of
momentary distractions.
and when it's
finally over
i want to lie in
the bosom of satisfaction
with you
**resting comfortably
on my chest.** ♥

Her Voice

the telephone rings…
its**her voice**
on **the line.**

my heart
took flight
and
suddenly i hear
the sounds of
Cherubims and Seraphims.

i am in
celestial paradise.
i just **get hooked**
on the sound
of her voice,
it does **unnatural things**
to me.

the stock value
of **my telephone**
rises
when she is
on the other end
of the line.

i am willing
to invest
my life savings
in phone credit
just to hear
her voice.

r. A. bentinck

Intuition

i spotted
her smile
in the distance
and it **vanquishes**
the gloom of my day.

her words
were beams
of **sunlight**
in a cloud
decorated sky.

she took possession
of my hands
while we walked
wordlessly.

somehow
she knows
when **words**
are best placed
in time out. ♥

Smile

in
a darkened world

your smile
is
the open window

that
lets in
the light
and
fresh air. 🖤

r. A. bentinck

February 14th

long after
the taste of chocolate
fades from the tips
of your tongue,
my love for you
would still be around.

long after
picked red roses
wither and die
my love for you will still
be alive.

this love
will continue
to withstand the test of
cold shoulders,
silent treatments,
arguments and disagreements.
this love will continue
to fight through
tough days,
tough weeks,
tough months,
and tough years.

this love
has staying power!
long after
scented candles
burn out
this love will continue
to shine brightly. ♥

If I Could

if only
i could possess
the power to
turn back time.

i would devise
a solid plan
to meet you
so much sooner.

i would **recoup**
the **wasted time**
so that we have
more time
to be **with each other.** 🩶

r. A. bentinck

Her Eyes

her eyes,
enchanting,
to say the least.
one look,
one playful glance,
one innocent stare,
and they abduct my emotions
to a place of blissful stupidity.

she makes me
smile **uncontrollably**
and my heart plays
a samba beat in my chest.
she often asks what wrong with me,
but **i am not crazy.**
it's the potent combination
of **her angelic eyes**
and **mischievous smile**
that floors me every time.

her eyes, charming,
captivating, fascinating.
one look, one shy glance
and i'm swept away.

she doesn't know
and she will never
understand the power of her eyes,
she never takes
the time to see
the **unspeakable beauty**
in her eyes. ♥

Valentine Poetry

For Everything

for all the smiles
you gave to me,
for all the smiles
you made me smile,
thank you, baby.

for the love you give unselfishly,
for the times **you were my eyes**
when i was too blind
to see, **thank you.**

for the meaning
you brought to my life,
for all the joys
you added to my existence,
for **seeing the best in me.**
thank you, baby.

for putting up with me
throughout my insensitivities
and uncertainties,
thank you.
your **tenderness**
surrounds me in a special way.

you found my faith
and give it back to me.
for all that you have done
for me, **i am grateful.**
thank you, baby,
for believing in me.
my life is better because **you are**
a part of it, thank you, baby. ♥

r. A. bentinck

The Smile

your smile, so serene.
so soothing.

your eyes afire
my burning desire.

from across the shop counter
i feel bliss.

i always look forward
to your
welcoming smile.

those twinkling eyes
come alive.
i'm hypnotized,
emotion wise.

it is my simply reply
to
your beautiful smile. ♥

Valentine Poetry

This Morning

this morning i awoke,
you were the first thing
on my mind,

you were **the sunrise**
spreading your **golden rays**
across the sky.

this morning i woke up,
and **you were**
the fresh rose in my garden,

your tender petals blowing
in **the cooling breeze,**
your **celestial** fragrance
gently fills
the morning scent.

this morning i woke up,
and memories of you
and
your ever-glowing beauty
enfolds me like
the fresh morning breeze-
cool, gentle,
soothing and refreshing.

this morning i woke up
and you were
the essence of life. ♥

r. A. bentinck

Valentine Poetry

Chapter Four: Hardcore Loving

r. A. bentinck

Valentine Poetry

Forgiven

no, you are not still
a part of me
because of **my stupidity.**

you are here
because i choose
to love you.

you have **cheated**
and in the eyes
of the **sinless lovers**
it is **your greatest sin,**

but i choose to forgive you
because i have walked
that road before,
i have traversed
the valley of the tempted
i have **given in**
to **my weak ways.**
i know the reality well.

no, you are not still
a part of me
because of my stupidity.
you are here because
i choose to love you

and **if the night**
should turn to day,
a lot of **finger-pointers**
and accusers
will be put to **shame.** 🩶

r. A. bentinck

From the Valleys of Love

when the **honeymooning phase
fades**
we must face the reality.
and it is only then
the true test begins.

**is this a lusting
or
a loving thing?**

when the new love
**excitement
gradually disappears**
and we both return
to default
then is when
we get to know
if this

**is this a lusting
or
a loving thing?**

when life throws
**explosives
at love's doorstep**
and hearts get
tattered and broken
only then we will
get to know

**is this a lusting
or**

a loving thing?

when temptations
makes repeated
and disguised visits
and **hearts and knees
get weak**
then we will get
to see if this
 is this a lusting
or
a loving thing? 🖤

r. A. bentinck

Ghetto Love

i took a bullet
today
but **i didn't shed
a tear,**

but your **comforting
words,** and **healing ways**
brought a flood
of **tears to my eyes**
and hope
to my injured psyche.

they try
to kill me
but your **love
saved me.**
they judge me
but you love me,
they will never understand
why you continue
to care because **they don't know**
what we share.
their samurai sword looks
sometimes **cut me deeply**
but your **unconditional love
heals me.**

they try to hurt me
but your love **restores me.**
they continue to
judge me
while **you keep on
loving me.** ♥

Valentine Poetry

Loving the Hurt Away

i come from a place of hurt
and very few can
empathise with **my pain.**

but you,
you continually seek ways
to help me
get by,
cope,
survive,
heal.

disguised love
shattered me into
so many pieces
i am still
sorting through
the puzzle
to put me **back**
together again.
you don't always
understand **my tears,**
but you are always there
to **wipe them away.**
it's not easy being with me
but you choose
to stick by me
when so many others leave.

i come from a place
of hurt and
God knows how
i try every day,

r. A. bentinck

but sometimes
the **flashback**
and **memories**
always have it their way.

i am not easy to be around
but you are always there
with **a supporting love**
that keeps my head above
the waters that seek
to constantly drown me.

at times
i wished
you would leave
so you can **preserve
your sanity,**
but you never do and
that fortifies my love
for you.
i come from **a place of
broken**
and very **few**
would be able to **survive**
my pain
but **your good intentions**
and **love-filled ways**
is the **glue**
that keep **my piece together.** ♥

Valentine Poetry

These Streets (Raggamuffin Love)

these streets
will never take **the place**
of you.

these streets
will never be more important
than you.

these streets
will never bring me warmth
like you do.

these streets
will never bring me comfort
the way you.

but these streets
is where i make a living.

these streets
is where i hustle
to survive.

these streets
is where i have to walk
because sometimes
life puts you
on these streets. ♥

r. A. bentinck

Forbidden Love

your mama and papa
will gladly use
their holy cross
to shave
my dreadlocks,
and **exorcise**
the perceived **demon
out of me,**

just because you
are **in love with me.**

but you see me
under a different light,
you know me
like few do,
so you keep on
loving me

while they chastise
and ridicule me,

and if they could have
gotten away with it
they would have **crucified
both of us**
in the name of the lord.

all because they see
what we have as **sinful.** 🩶

Dangerous

she knows how to love
unconditionally.
and **when she loves
she loves strongly,**

but **don't play with
her heart**
because you will
**resurrect
the street** in her.

the same knife
she is good with
in the kitchen
she can use to
cut you in your sleep.

she has never been
to the shooting range
but **she is very skilled**
with an **illegal gun.**
if you love her
don't play with
her heart.
she can flip
from being **a lady**
to a **ghetto Pitbull
in a skirt** in seconds. ♥

r. A. bentinck

One Night Dilemma

you made me
fall for you,
hard.

is this a love
that last beyond
tomorrow
or
it's **just mine** for
tonight?

you made me
fall for you,
hard.

now i sense
this will not last
beyond **tonight,**
my foolish heart
should **take the blame.** ♥

Valentine Poetry

Locked Up

from quality time
to jail time
in the **sexy wink**
of **an eye**.

your **love is rationed**
by limited time,
a **bulletproof glass,**
an **old fashioned telephone**
and **prison officers**
watching your heartbeat.

desiring eyes and
tempting smile
wilts under the realization
that **innocence means**
nothing in this
justice system.

from quality time
to **jail time**
in the sexy wink
of an eye. 🖤

r. A. bentinck

The Meaning of Love

love was just
a **word** to me
until you came along
and **gave it meaning.**

i don't have to come
to you with **a fake smile**
on my face
and my **ready hands**
on the **trigger.**

you showed me how
to trust again,
you **loved** me and
all **my thuggish ways.**

you don't **judge**
or **bug** me,
you **respect the street**
in me.
love was just a word
until **you showed** me
its true meaning. ♥

Uncertainty

i don't quite
understand you
and it's even more
difficult to read whats
hidden in your **heart.**

i don't know where i stand
with you.
i feel your love
but i don't hear your love.

every time i think
about you
it makes me want you **more.**

i can feel your love,
i can see your love,
but i don't
hear your love
for me.

r. A. bentinck

Ride or Die Love

you touch me,
you touch her.

you **hurt me,**
you **hurt her.**

when we are under attack
we are **an inseparable team.**

we **ride these** streets
together,
and we **don't mind dying**
in these streets
together.

we don't talk
about our guns
but **we know**
our guns.
we war against
anything that messes
with our love. ♥

Uncompromising

he doesn't play
by **society's rule.**

he is not easily fooled.

he doesn't follow
the **gullible masses.**

he is not a sheeple.

but you will be **hard-pressed**
to **question the tender love**
in his heart **for his girl.** ♥

r. A. bentinck

Gangster Loving

she looked in the eyes
with **steely** confidence
and made her opinion
clear:

if you are riding,
baby, i am riding
with you. we are in
this thing together.

love is not only a
three-letter words,
it's the reassuring
commitment
knowing someone
has your back
no matter what. ♥

Valentine Poetry

Chapter Five: Teen Love

r. A. bentinck

Finally

i thought about it
all day and late at night.

i tried my skilled
and cunning tactics
to no avail.

she knew
i wanted it
for so long.

yet she denied me
kept it from me.

then one day,
after i gave up
on so many
of my failed schemes

she came to me
and
kissed me
the way my dogs
licks me
after being away
all-day. 🖤

r. A. bentinck

She Is

she is the reason
i fall asleep
with my phone
in my hand.

she is the reason
why my heart
skips a beat
unexpectedly.

she is responsible
for my sudden
stuttered speech
and **nervous twitches.**

she is the first
and last thought
on my mind
each day.
this girl
means so much
to me
in so many ways. 🖤

Criminals

i must admit
we are **both criminals.**

she sneaked up
on me
stole my heart,
and
i stole hers
just to get even.

now we walk around
hand in hand
smiling with contentment
at our illicit deed.

r. A. bentinck

Fear

away from you,
there is so much
i have to say to you
i can fill a novel
with all the words.

in your presence
fear staples my lips
and **tie my tongue**

and i am frozen in
the moment
losing all of my
built-up heat. ♥

Fell

i fell and bumped my head
on her stunning
artificial beauty.

she controlled me
like a remote-controlled toy.

**i went to the cliff's edge,
repeatedly**
to satisfy her unquenchable needs.

she made a fool out of me
just because i was too blind to see,

too gullible to be objective
and to dazed to see reality. 🖤

r. A. bentinck

Foolish Heart

my heart knows
we've been **here before**.

we both know
the sensations that
preceded the temptations.

we know the pain
that follows
the disappointment
which coarse through
every vein in my being.

we both know **the salty taste**
of the torrential tears.
yet it gave in
to her lure.
so here we are again
in heartbreak timeout
tending to bruises
and **sealing up the crack**
on a worn-out heart. ♥

In My Dreams

in my dreams
she was **oh so real.**

she fulfilled my every need,
satisfied my large desire appetite,
took me to places
that made my heart galloped
in flower-filled meadows.

but in my waking reality,
she didn't know me.
she paid me no heed
she was just a fiction
of my lust-filled yearnings. 🩶

r. A. bentinck

Lion King

i am Simba
and she is
my Nala.

ours is a story
one of innocence
and adventure.

lost and found
triumph over
adversities.

despite where life
takes us
she will always
have a place in my heart. ♥

Perception

my classes are not
the same
if she is not in school.

my lunch is not as appetizing
if she is not
in the opposite chair.

my phone notifications
are not as important
if her name doesn't appear.

friends are just props
i used to kill time
until she arrives.

i can lay in bed
all the time
with her memory
keeping me company.

r. A. bentinck

Puppy Love

i want her to be
the one who wears
my hoodie
when it gets cold
while snuggling up
next to me.

i want to borrow
her pen
when mine
runs out of ink.

i want her
to gossip and giggle
with her friends
when i pass by
with her honeyed smile.
i want to sneak up
behind her
with a passionate embrace
and whisper
candy words in her ear. ♥

Rebel

it seems like
the entire school is
against me.

but she doesn't give
a rat's ass!
this is all that
matters to me.

i don't need
the entire school
or the world
to love me.

as long as
she is with me
i am cool with
whatever the world
throws at my feet.

r. A. bentinck

Smitten

she arrested my
common sense and sensibility.

being flustered
became my new normal.

friends started highlighting
a level of stupidity i didn't see.

she became the supreme thought
in my waking hours.

she controlled the rapidity
of my heartbeat with her presence.

it seems everyone saw
my helpless state except me. ♥

Unexpected

somewhere
along the way
amidst all the
uncontrolled laughter,

the friendly conversations
that seems to
never end;

somewhere
among the unexplained
fights
and silly disagreements,

somewhere
between the corny jokes
we were prepping
the fertile soil
for love to grow
and flourished.
one day the bloom
caught us by
sweet surprise.

our lips parted,
tongues greeted,
and hearts raced. ♥

r. A. bentinck

Pixie Dust

there was something
about Stacy
that transcended normality.

her every action
stimulated me in ways
that was new to me,

every word that
flowed from her supple lips
left me drooling for more,

everything she did and say
contain lavish amount
of pixie dust. ♥

Valentine Poetry

Chapter Six: You Are The Reason

r. A. bentinck

Valentine Poetry

Fall Asleep

you can fall asleep
in my arms
baby, there is **no**
need to explain
your tiredness.

and if your dreams
are scary
callout my name
i will be here
to wake you
from the nightmare.

i am here for you
during the
your **high tides**
and during
your **low tides.**

on sunny days
and rainy nights
i promise
i will here
whatever it takes. ♥

r. A. bentinck

Matching

i'm not coming,
armed with sweet and
seductive words
and cliché phrases,
only.

i come
with matching actions
and effort
to make it all
an experience
for you to savour.

i'm greater than
a **one-dimensionality**
masterpiece. 🩶

Illuminated

you walked into
my life
and **turned on the light.**

you made me see
the light.
you made things
brighter.

there are **butterflies
in abundance**
every time
your eyes meet mine.

when our lips meet
there is a feeling
that's **so divine**
i am often left **searching
for words**
to **explain the sensations.**

r. A. bentinck

Heaven Knows

heaven knows
what they placed in you
when **you were created.**

it's not prudent of me
to try and **makes sense of
it all.**

what i will do
is
take the **time
to enjoy it all,**

heaven already knows. ♥

Ever-Present

with your name
on the tip
of **my tongue**

and you
in the center
of **my mind**

there is **seldom**
a dull moment
in my life
at this time. 🩶

r. A. bentinck

Blowing Kisses

i love it when you
blow me kisses
on the
wings of a smile.

i love the click
of **your heels**
when you turn and saunter
away
mischievously. ♥

No Rules

this is tantamount to
starvation
with so much
sacrificed time
between us

on an occasion like this
we don't play
by the known rule book.

let
creativity
and
adventure
take the reign
and guide our
primal instinct. ♥

r. A. bentinck

Your Kisses

your kisses make me
plea to the breeze
for its **cooling balm.**

you send **my temperature**
to **sweltering** levels
at a time when
the **northern wind**
bids us au revoir.

you turn **my mouth**
into **an oasis**
that doesn't satisfy
my thirst for **you.**

despite the prevailing
circumstances i am still
a glutton for your kisses.

what have you done
to me? **when you kiss me**
up and down
my senses get tossed into
a **blender**
and **i am at your mercy.** ♥

Distance Lovers

even though we are
miles apart
and you still find
a way
to surmount
oceans and seas
to be close
to my heart.

this distance,
is a **true testimony**
to how far your love
travels **to be**
with me. 🖤

r. A. bentinck

The Patient Lover

insatiable desires
and flaring lust **yaps**
at me **daily,**

but i will go to the gym
to **strengthen** and build
my patient muscles.

they are weak
but i am not going
to **give in.**

i will wait
until you are ready,
in body,
in mind,
and in spirit.
i will wait for you.

i will **not rush**
nor force you
into doing anything
you are not ready
to do.
i will not make you
uncomfortable.

i will wait
for your readiness,
it's worth it. ♥

Valentine Poetry

One Day

one day
there will be **no more
distance.**

one day
we will be in the same **house
we call home.**

one day
you will be **waking up**
to me daily.

one day
we won't have to look at the clock,
because we have limited time.

one day
the plane ticket will be
one way.
one day 🖤

r. A. bentinck

Notifications

in a barrage of technological
attention grabbers

you are my favorite
notification.

in a multitude
of **ringtones**

it's yours that brings
the mile-wide smile

and **a glow to**
my **once dull eyes.**

Valentine Poetry

Perfection

i am not looking for perfection.
i looking **for persistence.**

there will be
difficult days ahead
but if we are persistent
we will overcome them
together.

i am not looking for perfection
i am looking **for consistency.**

if we do the things daily
that **fosters love,**
that **restores love,**
that **ignites the fire,**
that **preserve love,**
we will have little
to fear,
we will have a strong foundation
always.

i am not looking for
social media **glitz and glamour**
nor do I want
the perfect pictures to post,

i want true happiness,
mutual respect and **honour**
behind closed doors.

i am not looking
for perfection. 🖤

r. A. bentinck

Goodbyes

saying goodbyes
use to be **a no-brainer**
for me.

ever since you came
into my life
goodbyes are **not**
the **same anymore.**

goodbyes are now
complicated and contradicting.

saying goodbye
to you
brings **a lump**
to **my throat,**
a **sad beat** to
my heart,

excited anticipations
of seeing you again,
and a **longing** to be
with you in so many ways.
my **goodbyes**
 aren't the same **anymore.**

Valentine Poetry

Chapter Seven: Falling For You

r. A. bentinck

Animality

damn,
i want you
unrestrictedly.

i want you like
unashamed animals,
in the wild.

damn
i want to hear
your unmuffled screams
shaking the dried leaves
off the sturdy tree.

the thought of
having you
without restraints
is intoxicated. 🖤

r. A. bentinck

Rainy Thoughts

i can hardly
see through
my misty window
let alone
see
the distant trees.

it is
cold,
windy,
and a multitude is
pelting down
ice crystals from above.
in the midst
of the shivering weather
a warm thought
comforted me.
this is
the ideal weather
to scamper
in the rain with you.

to play like
carefree kids
on vacation.
i pressed my nose
against the fridge like window
and whispered:
where are you, baby?
i want to run
in the rain with you. 🩶

Valentine Poetry

My Favourite Things

painting that sweet smile
on your glowing face,

touching your funny spot
and hearing you go
crazy with laughter,

soothing your tension
with **slow fingers
on your baby skin,**

sipping sweetness
from your lips
at every convenient moment,

lazing the worries of
the day away in your company,
getting lost in your eyes
while your fragrance
serenade me to a natural high,
listening to the wisdom
that emanates from the words
that flows from your mouth,

holding your hands
just to experience
your spiritual vibes. ♥

r. A. bentinck

The Scent of a Woman

i am a bloodhound
with images of **you**
on my mind

and the scent
of **your sweetness**
in the halls of my nose.

i want to lose my way
in the fields
of your fragrance

and be found
in **the paradise of**
your sweetness. ♥

Legality

is this really
legal?

she is sending
me
these carnal pictures
now i am in
a vulnerable state.

Each
new batch
weakens
my vulnerability meter.

hair-raising,
toe-curling,
lip-biting,
spine-tingling,
imagination accelerating
images…
excuse me
while **i search for
my breath…**
damn!
today
she was picture
teasing me
and
it wasn't funny.

i need to consult
my the legal text about
how lawful

r. A. bentinck

it is to expose
someone
to such mind-altering
experience

when they are
in a vulnerable state.
damn,
she is beyond sexy! ♥

Valentine Poetry

Unfriendly

the morning weather
is frigid and unkind

i lay bright-eyed
and **uncaring**
to the sounds
the crowing cocks,
the high-spirited birds,

and
the ominous
tick-tock,
tick-tock,
tick-tock,
of the clock

as it squanders minutes
off of my work morning.
i am safely
wrapped up
in the warmth
of my baby's arm
and in no hurry
to go anywhere.
i count the grains
in the ceiling wood,
i twiddle
my blanket warm toes
as i fine-tune
my ignoring skills.

i am
a rebel

r. A. bentinck

this morning
and
time
and
my boss
is going to have
to deal with it
today. ♥

Connecting Conversations

with so much time
spent in conversations
unconsciously
we are constructing
emotional explosives.

all this
pent-up passion
and
surplus of
romantic intensity
is going to
ignite
when we finally meet.

there is no way
to predict
if we have
what it takes
to control
and satiate
our insatiable hunger.

r. A. bentinck

Window Curtains

come on in
and leave the world
outside the door.

close
the window curtains
and
starve the prying eyes.

let's prep ourselves
for a feast
made **for the starving.**

let our sounds
of satisfaction
resuscitate
the imaginations
of the dying. 🖤

Valentine Poetry

Word Search

i want to find
the kinds of words
that reaches you
where you are
but elevate you
to places you have
never been to before.

i want to find
quality words
that sets your
mind and body
at ease,

where you are comfortable
with stepping into
the unknown with
the level of confidence
that stuns your
shy and reclusive self.

i want to find
the words that **open
the reservoir**
of your honey ways.
i want to find
the types of words
that reaches you
where you are
and take you
to places **beyond
your imagination.** 🖤

r. A. bentinck

Slow

with you
i wanna take it
very slow.
i can rush
into the core
of **your sweetness**
but i won't.

i find
a certain
delicious pleasure
in delay gratification
when i am with you.

i find delight
in taking it slow
when it comes to you.

i take pride
in dismantling
your inhibitions

and watch a whole
new you unfold
moment by moment. ♥

3 A.M.

it's you again,
roaming the halls
of my mind
dropping crumbs of
inspirations
every step of the way.

you are disturbing
my restful sleep.

your inspirations are so
fresh and tempting
i dare not give into
the thought of going
back to rest.

i rolled off the bed
with uncertain feet
while the words
fall to the floor.
when my fingers hit
the keyboard
sleep was vanquished
by the effortlessness
of your imagery, that flowed. 🩶

r. A. bentinck

Slow Kisses

i want
to make
slow kissing
with you
a study
in the essence of
seduction.

i want
to study your
cupid's bow as we stroll in
for the first experience.

i want to trace
your vermillion borders
and spend some
extra in their **supple zones,**
just to feel every
subtle detail.

i want to enjoy
the **sensations**
that comes with
feeling every tubercle
on your top and bottom lips.
i want to get lost
in the **euphoria**
of your kisses. ♥

Dress to Kill

she pirated my smile
as soon as she stepped
in the room.

my emotions,
was at the mercies
of her every stride,

my imagination,
deserted me
to be in her company.

my eye caressed
every **glamorous curve**
of her shapely
masterpiece.
she wore her
sleek black dress
like a **seductive empress.**

r. A. bentinck

Sun Kissed

she kissed me like
the morning sun
and
my day became
brighter
and
warmer.

her **moist warm lips**
was breakfast
to my yearnings. 🖤

Chapter Eight: The Look Of Love

r. A. bentinck

Valentine Poetry

Heartbeat

send me your heartbeat
so i can fall asleep

send me your heartbeat
to set my mind at ease

send me your heartbeat
so it can **lighten my day**

send me your heartbeat
it's the music i wanna hear. ♥

r. A. bentinck

Thoughts

i was just sitting here
thinking
about your baby kisses
and those
teddybear embrace

and
my **face started glowing**
with a smile. ♥

Heated Smile

like a helpless moth
to **your enticing flame**
the heat in your smile
draws me near
and **drive me bonkers.**

i am captured
can't you see it
in my eyes
and my uncharacteristic
mannerism.

ooh baby,
don't stop…
smile for me
some more.
come closer so i can
feel the full intensity
of the heat.

come closer, baby
closer
brand me
with **your smile.**

r. A. bentinck

Always

i know it won't
always be smiley
and cuddly moments.

there will be
challenging times,
rainy days,
and days out in
the **frigid weather,**

but

always know
you **will always,**
always
have my love
and respect.
you may walk
in the rain just to hide
your tears

but i will always
be there
to wipe your
fears and pains away.
always.

you can always rely on
these shoulders
to lean on
and my tender touch
will never be too far away.
remember when

it all gets too much
i will be here
to help you
through it all.

you are an
important ingredient
in my life. ♥

r. A. bentinck

Rainy Rhythms

a raindrop orchestra,
a warm bed,
cuddly embrace,
and
nowhere to go
in a hurry.

perfect.

we sprawled out
like lions
on the prairie
after a large and
satisfying meal.

the torrential drumming
on the tin roof
is the kind
of sound that
does something
to our sensual strings.

we **toss our imaginations**
to the creative wild
and with love in our arms
and extra privacy
under a comfy blanket
there is not telling
the places **we will explore.** ♥

Relaxation (food for the soul)

comfortable
with the morning's laziness
instinctively
we nestled
into the comfort
of each other's arm.

no need for conversation
we just listen
to each other's breath
and
nature's morning choir.

we froze in the comfort
of **body heat**
only twitching
for a lazy stretch
here and there

while we waste
the morning time
away without
giving a damn. ♥

r. A. bentinck

The Model Student

i will take the time
to read and understand
your mind,

uncover what makes you
tick
find out what makes you
quietly coax
your **shyness to away.**

i am in this class
for mastery,

i will develop the mindset
of a PhD student
whose goal
is to graduate
with honours.

i want to be proficient
at **knowing**
how to please you
in every way. ♥

I Will Wait

if you are
not ready
i will wait for you.

i will wait
for your mood
to change,
i will wait
for you to get
to that place,
i will wait on you.

if you are not ready
i will wait
for you.
i won't be
impatient
i will wait
on you. ♥

r. A. bentinck

Lullabies

pitter-patter
pitter-patter
pitter-patter
on the tin roof
and on
the cashew tree leaves.

we lay at ease
in **the rhythms**
of **the rain.**

mother nature
knows
how to romance
our mind and body.

pitter-patter
pitter-patter
pitter-patter
on the tin roof
and on
the cashew tree leaves.

we give to calling
of the rhythms
of the raindrops.

the raindrops
create **a soothing melody**
taking our mind
and body to a
celestial place. ♥

Valentine Poetry

Teach Me

i may not be familiar
with
your love language
but i sure
would like
to **master it**

teach me, please.

teach me the **things
that pleases you**
the most,

teach me the things
that always
takes you to the
precipice of satisfaction.
teach me
in the mornings,
teach me in the
evenings, too.

teach me
even when
i am slow
and unwilling
teach me.

teach me
what i need know
to **make you happy.**

when you are

r. A. bentinck

feeling blue,
tell me what
you are going through
teach me.

watch me take notes,
watch me improve,
watch me experiment,
just because
i want
to do well enough
to please you.

teach me, please. 🖤

The Stars

did you see that
shooting star?

the night may be dark
but we can search
for constellations
and look
for **shooting stars.**

bring along
a bottle of
our liquid cheerleader
for **added company.**

with our backs
to earth and
our eyes fixated
on the speckled blanket
above
let's savour
the grandeur
**of mother nature's
awesomeness.**

r. A. bentinck

Thoughts of You

i was just
sitting here thinking
about
your baby kisses
and those
teddy-bear embrace,

and
my face started glowing
with
a mile-wide smile.

the memories
of your voice
does something
that tingles me
in secret places. ♥

Valentine Poetry

Inexplicable

we didn't see
this coming.
and **the more**
i think about it
the more its
doesn't seem
logical.

what did it trigger?
why us?
where is it taking us?
will it get more intense?
how will we cope?

thoughts followed **words,**
words accompanied **emotions,**
words toyed with **hidden yearnings**, words blended
with actions
to satisfy unquenchable desires. 🖤

r. A. bentinck

Changes

you brought so much
when you
stepped
into my life.

i am alive now,
but once ago
i was dead.

i see
hope and dreams
in places where
i once saw
death and decomposition.

i am energetic now
once ago
i was listless.

i am learning
to swiftly adopt
to **the life-altering changes**
you bring. ♥

Valentine Poetry

Chapter Nine: Mellow Moods

r. A. bentinck

Mornings Of Memories

there is nothing to compare
to waking up with
the fond memories
of her affectionate kisses
on my mind.

there is a freshness
that comes from reminiscing
about her delightful smile.

her morning memories
wake me up in
the sweetest of ways daily.
good morning,
morning memories. ♥

r. A. bentinck

Complicated

my body
pressed against yours
and
breathing has becomes
as complicated
as a science equation

that i must solve
in a minute.

there is
so much electricity
flowing through
our bodies
we can easily
light up the capital city.
i feel so many things
all at once
i want to say
so much
but my words
deserted me.

it has only
been a minute
yet **it feels like
an eternity.**

what are you
doing to me? 🖤

Valentine Poetry

Heartbeat

send me your heartbeat
so i can **fall asleep**

send me your heartbeat
to set my **mind at peace**

send me your heartbeat
so it can **lighten my day**

send me your heartbeat
it's the music i wanna hear. 🖤

r. A. bentinck

Chocolate Lollipops

sweetness with a twist.
here are some
heart-shaped,
flower-decorated
lollipops

just because
i want to be different.

here is **my sweetness**
with a twist
just because i want
to see you smile. 🖤

You Are

you are
that flower upon which
the butterfly
rests
it's sore feet
and **tired wings.**

you are
that selected rose
whose hidden sweetness
the hummingbird,
skilfully pauses
to sip.

you are
the shaded tree
under whose trunk
the tired farmer
seek refuge
from
the unforgiven midday sun.

you are the leaf upon which
the **morning dew**
lingers a little longer.

you are that soothing voice
amidst
the chaos and
the confusion
of the moment.
i see your qualities
in everything. 🖤

r. A. bentinck

Kiss Me Again

good morning greetings
with **rose-petal-like kisses.**
it's one of the surreal
ways of waking up,
besides you.

kiss me again.

tongues frolic
while we say our parting
goodbye with a kiss as we leave
for the day's work.
it tastes so good.

kiss me again.
afternoon kisses
as we **welcome
each other home**
from a labourious day
at the office.
i miss the moments
away from you.

kiss me again.
evening kisses
as we relax
with engaging gossip.
it feels wonderful
chilling with you.

kiss me again.

goodnight kisses

can be so **unpredictable.**
they unearth **hidden gems,**
takes us to **insatiable places,**
open perspirations glands
and makes us loose
our sense of time and space.
goodnight kisses are magical.
kiss me
again,
and
again
and
again…
kiss me one more time. 🖤

r. A. bentinck

Without Saying A Word

it's the energy in
your eyes
that electrify
my electric bulb smile.
you have an **amazing way**
of touching me
in tender places.

no words,
just your company.
No words,
Just your fragrance.
No words,
and i am
transported
to a serene place.
it's the **conversations,**
between our hearts
that reassures me
that i am safe
and **you** will never
let me hurt without
reaching out for me.
it's the silky touch
of your hands
that says to me
you will never let me
fall.

you say so much
to me **without saying**
a word. ♥

Valentine Poetry

Top Down

top-down on
the **lonely highway.**

a darkened night
and **your lighted smile.**

miles to go
but i don't mind.

you are cruising with me
and the feeling is irie. ♥

r. A. bentinck

Your Memories

on days when
the sun
hides its face
behind darkened clouds,

i reach for your
ever-present memories
and **the light**
finds its way
through the clouds
again. ♥

Rekindled

some days will be tough.
we might **become victims**
of **neglect** and **complacency**,
but that doesn't mean
the fire has been
extinguished.

let's look for that
small spark
that
warrior ember
that refuses
to give up despite
the unrelenting winds.

let's look for
the glimmer in
fading hope
let,s never give up
or give in.

let's fan vigorously
the **flames** that
still burn beneath
all the confusions and
distractions.
**let's rekindle
our love.** ♥

r. A. bentinck

Time Watcher

it's only when
i caught myself **watching
the time** and
marking the dates
on my calendar
that i realized
the magnitude of
how much i will
miss you.

your silly and
girlish ways,
your unexpected charm
and romantic ways,
your soothing presence
and switchblade
sense of humour.
baby, i am gonna miss you.

i will mark the date
and **count the time**
and even though
i will be back soon
baby, **i am still gonna
miss you.**
i hear them call my name
over the p.a. system
but i don't want to leave
but duty calls.

the thought of not seeing you
for months
weights heavier on my shoulders

than the overweight carryon
i dragged unwillingly
behind me.
baby, i am already
missing you.

i paused on the tarmac
to pick out your smiling face
and **waving hands**
from a sea of faces
with mixed emotions.

the sights and **inaudible sounds**
from the departure lounge
hit me harder.

the warm smile and
welcome onboard greeting
meant nothing to me,
i am missing,
my baby. 🩶

r. A. bentinck

Love From A Distance

my spirit emerges
from the superficial bondage
of the mind
and soared beyond
the limitations of:
time,
space,
distance,
and location.

it merged with
the universal mind
and we begin to speak.

we speak of love,
the love we have,
unconditional love
from a distance.
i heard a song of love that said,
i am in you and you in me.
it tells me that there
are times we meet
telepathically.
and we do the things
we once did and more
it tells me that,
there are times
you walk the streets
and think of me.
it tells you that i do
the same too.
it tells me that

Valentine Poetry

there are times
when certain sounds
and fragrances
just spark thoughts
of us.

it tells you,
the same is true for me too.
it tells me that
though our physical meetings are
too often brief;
the moments are sacred
and self-healing.

it tells you our love still grows-
from a distance.
i watched the silver moonrise
tonight
and i see you in it.
it radiates your kisses
and warm embrace.
the light caresses my body
and melts the darkness away.

the feelings it brings
tells me
that love from a distance
is no lesser love.
i spread my window wide and
invited the moon inside.
the light is warm and cozy,
it lay next to me
in the vacant space
of my bed.

it soothes me

r. A. bentinck

to a peaceful sleep.
slowly,
i drifted into blissful rest
with
thoughts of you
on my mind. 🩶

Sweet Talk You

may i have a moment
of your time?
i want to sweet talk you.
i want to tell you
about the joys you bring me.

may i speak to you
away from prying eyes?
i want to sweet talk you.
i want to tell you how much
you mean to me,

may i have a few minutes
of your precious time?
i want to sweet talk you.
i want to sit in
the company of
your radiant smile
and tell you stories while
i get lost in your angelic eyes.
may i have a moment
with you?
i just want
to sweet talk you.

r. A. bentinck

Innocently

the way you call my name
the way that you smile
the way you embrace me.
unwittingly,
they all turn me on.

your playful kisses
on my cheek,
your childish grin
the simple touch of your hands
sends a current through me.
your simple ways
seduce me.

your caring personality,
your warmth and generosity,
your unexpected humour
and joy-filled laughter.
it all teases me.
the **rolling of your eyes,**
the way **you walk away**
whenever i irritate you,
your brave attempts
at giving me the silent treatment;
it's all attractive to me.
all that you do
so innocently
makes you even more
attractive to me. ♥

Valentine Poetry

Chapter Ten: A Love Supreme

r. A. bentinck

The Sweetness From Your Lips

i saw your lips
for the first times
and started
salivating over
it's perceived
sweetness
softness
succulence
and
sumptuousness.

the first time
we kissed
i tried to kiss
the honey
from your lips
and got addicted.
today,
i'm a happy lip addict
who has no problem
getting his daily fix
of kissing sweetness
from your lips. 🖤

r. A. bentinck

Desirable

her silky voice
caress my auditory faculties
and
send shivers
through my senses.

her bright
and
inviting eyes
call out to my soul
bringing a fond smile
to my face.

heavenly scents
whisk me off to
a celestial place
where
she satisfies
my every fantasy. ♥

Valentine Poetry

In Your Eyes

that quiet look
in your eyes,
the one that
whips up storms
on the inside
sending my imagination
crazy.

that piercing look
in your eyes
that sends quivers
through my sensual faculties
leaving me with
uncontrollable urges.
that baby look in your eyes,
the one that
say more than
words allow
with it, i can sense
your unconditional love. 🩶

r. A. bentinck

Pee

i awake to her
adjusting to
a more comfortable
position on my chest.

the morning birds
were also up
they were being there
usual noisy self.

eyes still close
while my thoughts roamed.

her surprising snore
was greeted by
the calling of a need
to pee

i ignored it
once, twice,
but it kept getting
stronger.
i opened my eyes
and glanced
at her and her
face told the
entire story.

this pee is going to wait,
i don't want to disturb
her peace filled
rest on my chest. ♥

Late Night Dinner

with steamy lingerie
like that
let's do
late night dinner
under the stars,

where the still
of the night
sets the stage for
the soothing music of
the whispering wind.

i would love
to have
the pleasure of
dining with your smile
and enjoy the glow
of your excited eyes.

with erotic lingerie
like this
let's make plans
for a late-night dinner
under the watchful eyes
of winking stars. ♥

r. A. bentinck

I Wish

i wish
i could extend
the hands of time.

i wish
i could recoup
those wasted years.

i will
do whatever it takes
to prolong
these moments
in
your presence. ♥

In My Mind

in my mind,
i can taste
the essence
of your invitational lips.

in my mind
i can feel the warmth
of your enticing embrace
which quenches
my insatiable thirst.

in my mind
i can feel
electrifying sensations
seeping through my bone
making me excited.
in my mind
i can do
all the things
i want to do
to you
just because its
in my mind.

r. A. bentinck

She Said…

she messaged him
saying…
loving you more today
than yesterday
and
i know you'll give me
another reason today
to love you more
tomorrow.

little did she know
she just gave him
another reason
to love her even more. ♥

Tired Feet

i hope you are not
wearing stiletto heels
today
because you must have
tired feet by now.

why do i ask?

because you are
running around
in my mind
all-day like
a happy and playful child. ♥

r. A. bentinck

Oxygen

if it's not oxygen
why do i feel like
i'm going to die without it?

it's not like oxygen
but it feels like
i cannot survive without it.

if it's not oxygen
why i'm breathless
and suffocating?

it's not like oxygen
but i'm struggling
to breath without it.

i'm craving
your sweet lips against mine,
i'm craving
your warm and comforting caress.
it's not oxygen
but it seems like i need
your succulent kisses daily
just to stay alive. ♥

One More Time

i don't know
why you did
what you did
to me
but
do it to me
one more time.

i'm not sure
you know how
this makes me feel
so just
do it
one more time.
you have
unshackle my
unaddressed yearnings
please,
give it to me
one more time.

r. A. bentinck

Steppin' Out

i was her
bathroom valet
today.

i greeted her
with a rehearsed bow
and
my brightest smile
while extending
my towelled arm.

her
shower drenched body
was grateful
and
the thirsty towel
accepted each droplet
with glutton gratitude.

a surprised smile
warmed
her water masked face.

i knew
she wasn't
expecting this
level of service.

the tip i received
was passionately sumptuous,
now she has me
thinking
about firing my job. ♥

Valentine Poetry

Raindrops

we took
the bold steps…

after much
contemplation…

into
the unrelenting rain.

the forced adjustment
to the icy crystal drops
was swift.

then gradually
we found
our childlike feet
with splish-splash,
we frolicked,
we fooled around,
we created
pools and muddy puddles
of fun memories.

then we paused
in a soaked embrace
while our lips
gravitated
in search of
much needed warmth.

a few
jealous raindrops
sneaked in

r. A. bentinck

despite how tightly
the best efforts
of our lips.
i silently thought…
*um…this is more than
a threesome…*

we welcomed
the freshness
they added to
the moment's magic
and continued
undistracted. ♥

Valentine Poetry

Heading Home

the soothing sound
of her concerned voice
on the other
end of the line
was just
what i needed
to hear
stuck in
rush hour blues.

the orchestra
of impatient vehicles
and the smell of
tired asphalt
weight on the mind
after daily exposure.

but
i embrace
the comforting thought
that i am
on my way home

to the welcoming warmth
of a love
that will soon
make all of this
an ephemeral memory. ♥

r. A. bentinck

Chapter Eleven: Overjoyed

r. A. bentinck

Take Me There Again

take me to that place
where our breaths
become one,

take me to that place
where our lips
get entangled in a battle
that doesn't involve
retreating,
nor **surrendering.**

let's go to that place
where **our embrace**
is so close that even
the wind can't find
a way through.

take me to that place
where
we don't need words
to communicate
because
our body language
is so fluent that
interpretation
is instantaneous
and
all desires are satiated. 🩶

r. A. bentinck

Every-Day-Love

if i wait on a day
dedicated **to 'love.'**
to show you, **my love;**
to shower you
with love,
honey, you will be drowning
in love,
my love.

i do not want you to
fight to survive this love.
savour it…
moment-by-moment
by-moment…
i wait on no special day!
i will show you
e v e r y d a y.
in all ways.

for **this love is a journey**
cruising not speeding
gentle love
flowing not gushing.
each moment… golden, unique.
savour enjoy the flavour,
this is my love,
not
saint valentine's love.
this is **real love,**
everyday-love. ♥

Morning Glory

your lips as soft as petals
and your enticing fragrance
compels me to draw near.

your beauty
is as radiant as
the morning the sun.

your luscious breast
satisfies
my baby desires.

when my rugged hand's
gentle caresses
your sensual paradise
the warmth and tenderness
whisks me away in ecstasy.

each day
i am caught up in the reverie
of the honeyed recollections.
my morning glory
you mean the world to me.

r. A. bentinck

Sunrise

months ago, i left home,
there i knew
the names of flowers,
the names of
faces and places.

i ventured into this
'unknown world.'
and things covered me
in a different light.

for days,
i was gloomy
and then…
you appeared on my horizon.
the rays of
your golden smile
covered and comforted me,

you punctuated
my world
with colours once again:

warm and enlightening
yellows.
energizing and inviting
oranges.
sexy and stimulating
reds.
romantic and youthful
pinks.

cool and serene

blues.
healing and refreshing
greens.
spiritual and regal
purples.

powerful and elegant
black.
rich and sheltering
browns.
pure and innocent
whites.

now,
my world is like a fauvist canvas
filled with exuberant colours.
today i am feeling
the warmth of your rays
more than any other day.
now i know,
home is where
the sun rises. 🤍

your eyes,
the musical conductor,
orchestrating a melodic conversation
between two souls.

longing,
yearning,
thirsting,
desiring.

two spirits enjoying
the crescendo of feelings
once bottled up
from years of exile.
your eyes embrace me,
your eyes tease me,
your eyes speak to me,
your eyes
tell me that
love was always there
from the beginning.

now,
i can feel it all in
the crescendo of
love's afterglow. ♥

r. A. bentinck

Daybreak

morning dew tenderly kisses
the fresh vegetation outside
my opened window,
good morning.

a new day is dawning.
i awake with a blazing yearning,
my body keeps
calling,
calling,
calling for you.

in the cool of the morning
my body is burning up
because i am filled
with thoughts of you. ♥

Valentine Poetry

Her Kisses

her lips are smooth as butter,
and her tongue feels like rose petals.
she blows my senses away
and transcend me to a place where
nothing else mattered but kissing her,
being with her,
being held by her.

time has no meaning,
space no longer exists;
just this celestial moment
frozen in time.

her soft whispering voice
is the opiate
to my troubled mind.

delicate words of love
flows from her mouth and
she makes me feel like
the king of this world.

her closed eyelids speak of her
quiet satisfaction and
her relaxed body says volumes
of the moment.

her transcendental fragrance
captures my soul and reinforced
the essence of the moment.
her lips are smooth as butter,
and her tongue feels like rose petals
every time she kisses me. ♥

r. A. bentinck

I Want To Hold You

i want to hold you
like my favourite lily-
gently.
stroking you tenderly,
slowly, lovingly.

i want to play with your petals,
smell your enchanting fragrance,
let it linger on in my sense of smell.

i want to survey you slowly,
caress you slowly.

i want to hold you like my favourite lily-
savouring your delicate nature.
take you and please you.

i want to tickle your stamen
and see pleasure
glow-all-over your being.

i want to do the things
 that bring your
beautiful smile alive;
lighting up the atmosphere
with your compelling laughter.

i want to hold you like
my favourite lily-
please do not resist.
you will break your petals and
spoil your true essence. ♥

r. A. bentinck

Love's Crescendo Afterglow

at ease and at peace
in the effects
of love's afterglow.

your eyes beckon me
in dialogue,
loved-filled and
love-skilled.

they told me
that time passed
never dulled
the sharp edges
of the love that was
sparked years ago.

the whispers of
your batting eyelids
all décor in alluring lilac
draws me closer.
the warmth of your silky
sweat-drenched skin
captures my being.
your once well-groomed hair
now scatters in
romantic disarray.

the stillness of the night
creates an ideal backdrop
for this
quiet dialogue.
no words,
just feelings and gestures.

Caribbean Spice

there is something alluring about
your quiet exterior.
the coy smile
that softly fades away;
seeping into my being
acting as an aphrodisiac.

there is a richness in your
bustling strides as you quickly
glide by with a teasing smile
and twinkling eyes.

the sleekness
of your slender physique
coupled with your irresistible
ackee-coloured skin
makes lusting endearing.

you are like a classical jamaican
reggae love song
on a lover's holiday…
beres hammond's: 'no disturb sign.'
or
bob marley's: 'turn your lights down low.'

r. A. bentinck

Just One Thought

just the thought
of you
and the days seem
brighter.

just a fleeting thought
of you
and old familiar
music
seems refreshingly new.

just one thought
of you
changes everything. ♥

Morning Wish

may your day
be as bright as
your sunrise smile.

your moments
as excited as
your eyes
when you the recall
pulsating moments
we shared.

this is my
morning wish
for you. 🖤

r. A. bentinck

Flaming Desires

i want to
seduce you
to the edge of
your
flaming desires
where
heart-pounding sensations
steal
your breath away. ♥

Valentine Poetry

The Little Things

it's the little things
i wanna do with you.

i wanna run
and bathe
in the rain
with you.

i wanna stay
up all night
with you.

i wanna cook
nutritious meals
for you.
it's the little things

i wanna do for you.
i wanna hand-picked
roses
for you.

i wanna play
the fool
for you.
i wanna be
there for you.

i wanna do
all these little things
just for you. ♥

r. A. bentinck

Never Forget

as time goes by
and we **change**
and **rearrange,**

may we always
find a way
to **never lose sight**
of the spark
that first brought us
together.

as **our love**
goes through
the testing valleys
of life

may we always
find a way
to ignite those sparks
that caused us
to fall in love
the **first time.** ♥

Valentine Poetry

Chapter Twelve: Being With You

r. A. bentinck

Valentine Poetry

Cuddling

quick!
close the windows
and lock the doors
it's pouring
with a vengeance **outside.**

let's **slide under**
the **blanket,**
ensure our toes are covered,
let's cuddle and
and listen to
the rain's lullabies.

let's enjoy the jewels
of this **rare** moment.

r. A. bentinck

Touch

she looked me in the eye,
with **her mischievous smile**
and her **fingers wondered**
around my cheek.

she didn't speak
but she didn't have to
her **fingers said**
everything she felt
for me.

i closed my eyes
and **enjoyed** the
spectacular sensations
she generated
with **every electrifying**
touch. 🖤

Valentine Poetry

I See You

you are
that **flower** upon which
the butterfly
chooses to rest
it's sore feet
and tired wings.

you are
that selected rose
whose
hidden sweetness
the hummingbird
skillfully pauses
to sip.

you are
the **leaf** upon which
the **morning dew**
lingers a little longer.

you are
that **soothing voice**
amidst
the **chaos** and
the **confusion**
of the moment's **madness.**

i see you in everything. ♥

r. A. bentinck

Pillow Talk

spontaneous
but
refreshing.

we often **squander time**
in
engaging conversations.

there is **satisfaction**
and
strengthened **connections**
every time
we talk. ♥

Valentine Poetry

A Message a Day

a message a day
to **fuel our fire**
and **nourish**
what we share.

Monday's message
is to remind you of
how much i value
what we share.

Tuesday's message
is to **tease your senses**
into a **sensual frenzy.**

Wednesday's message
is to celebrate
our **daily blessings.**
Thursday's message
is to let you know
i'm still thinking
about you.

Friday's message
is to celebrate us.
Saturday's message
is just to **make you smile.**

Sunday's message
is to let you know
we have all day to ourselves
and there will be
no limitations
to what we say and do. ♥

r. A. bentinck

Half-Past Crazy

if only you could
see you
through my eyes,

maybe **you will assimilate**
why i am always
blissful whenever **i see you.**

if only just once
you can see you
through my eyes,

maybe then
you will **appreciate**
why i am
half-past crazy
over you. 🖤

You

you
you nourish
my daily thoughts,

you populate
my nightly dreams,

and you excite
my waking hours. ♥

r. A. bentinck

Pillows And Sheets

with a coy smile
plastered on her face
she declared,

you leave but your scent
lingers on my pillows and sheets.

i relive
every moment,
every emotion,
every sound,
like it's the real thing.

i know this might
sound eccentric,
but when you leave
i can still
feel you,
see you,
hear you,
taste you,
just from smelling
the enchanting fragrance
you leave on my pillows and sheets. ♥

Valentine Poetry

Because

i love you
the way i do
not just
because of how
i feel about you,

and how **my life**
has changed by having
you around,

but
because of **who**
i have become
by **being around you.** ♥

r. A. bentinck

Another You

i am pretty sure
life
doesn't have
another one
like you

waiting
to grace this earth
with your
incomparable presence. 🖤

Valentine Poetry

No More Fairytales

once upon a time
i use to **be excited about**
falling asleep
just to dream
about having **someone**
special in my life
to enjoy
the delicacies of life.

now, i loathe falling asleep
because **i found you**
and i don't
want **to miss out**
on the joy and beauties
of the waking hours
by wasting time
sleeping. ♥

r. A. bentinck

No Competition

i don't want to be
one of
your favourites.

**i don't want to be
an option**
when it comes to you.

i don't want to
give you a reason
to look back to compare.

i want to be
the **best you've
ever had.**

i want you to **forget
about past love**
and **bloom** in what
we have **now.** ♥

Electricity

behind every smile
you see **lighting up**
my excited **face,**

there is a thought
of **you**
in the background
providing electricity. 🤍

r. A. bentinck

35,000 Feet Up High-Cruising Altitude

thirty-five thousand feet up high
cruising in an iron bird,
and my heart is singing you a love song.

thirty-five thousand feet up high
and i can see and feel your smile,
and my heart beats an anticipatory melody.

thirty-five thousand feet up high
and am riding soft clouds of your
sweet memories.

thirty-five thousand feet up high
and **i have come to realize**
why this long journey is worth taking.
why the sacrifice is worth making.

thirty-five thousand feet up high
and i can see snapshots of your
memories through a small window space.
thirty-five thousand feet up high
and i close my eyes softly,
while a serene smile engulfs me
as i think about you at a cruising altitude,
of thirty-five thousand feet. ♥

Valentine Poetry

Chapter Thirteen: Love Test

r. A. bentinck

Valentine Poetry

Choices

listen baby,
at the end of the day
we can sit here
and **nourish**
the things that threaten
to put a dagger
through the heart
of what we cherish,

or

we can focus
on those things
**that bring a smile to
our faces,**
pour joy in our heart,
and give us
a realistic hope
for the future.

we always have choices,
let's **preserve** and
protect what we have built
over the years.

r. A. bentinck

Bedtime Stories

dear fairytales
you lied to us,
you made us believe
that it was all so easy.

dear romantic comedies
it's not always so funny
and the laughter
swiftly disappears like
a white rabbit
in a magician's hat.

dear music video
the skills of **bumping**
and grinding
didn't always translate
elsewhere. you made it
look **so seductively easy.**

dear bedtime stories,
you engraved in
our minds
false hopes and
lofty expectations.
dear mama,
i hate to admit it now
but so much of what
you said to me
that wasn't make-belief.
you were right
on so many levels. ♥

Valentine Poetry

Complicated

there were times when
i need you
and **you weren't there.**

there were times when
we had so much
to say
but the **words never came**.

there were times
when all we needed
was a little love and
understanding
but when we reach for them
we had none to share.

when you sewed
your lips shut
i realized that wishing
never allowed me
to **decipher** your
silent thoughts. 🩶

r. A. bentinck

Giving Up

should we give up breathing
because my nostrils
are **blocked by mucus?**

should we stop cooking
just because we got
one recipe went wrong
and spoil the entire dish?

should we give up
on the examination
just because we don't know
the answer to a few questions?

do we give up on each other
just because situations
aren't ideal?
no.
great relationship
are building on
a solid foundation
of compassion and understanding
it is often shaken
but **never grumbles.**
genuine love consist
of a foundation built
on the supportive columns
of two individuals who
understand
the power and strength
of togetherness. ♥

I Thought About It

i'm not going to
lie to you, baby
there were so many times
i thought about

**walking away,
running away,
starting over again
with someone new,**

but

i couldn't walk away
knowing
i was still truly in love
with you.

i couldn't run away
because so much inside
of me **said stay.**

that's why i'm still here today.
we both know
it wasn't easy
but we have to admit
holding on to each other
in the **adversarial winds**
was worth it. ♥

r. A. bentinck

It's Not Perfect

we are learning now
that is **not perfect**
and it will never be.

it's never the ways
they tell it
in **fairytales,**
romantic movies,
and **how-to books**
on love.

we have overcome obstacles,
survive stare-downs,
sparred with challenging times
and situations,
fought with each other,
and fight for each other.
we have learned to appreciate
that love requires
daily commitment and
a big and **forgiving heart.**

it's **such a small word**
with enormous demands.
easy to say
even when you are
faking it,

but so hard to show
when **it doesn't come**
from the depths of
the heart. ♥

Never Alone

i will not always
understand
the problems you face
but you can always
depend on me
to have a listening ear
whenever you want
to speak.

i will not always
be around
but know that
i will never let you
feel alone in my presence. ♥

r. A. bentinck

Temptation's Valleys

the wise ones say,
all relationships go through
the hell of
temptations,

the honeymoon phase,
they say,
spoil too many
because **it doesn't last**
forever.

but
the genuine relationships
and die-hard couples
survive it all.

they are the ones
who can look back
and smile
at how much they
learned from
and about each other
during the tough times. 🖤

Preserve The Garden

we didn't get this far
because it was all smiles and
laughter
daily.

we have survived
trying times,
had many silent conversations
with doubts and uncertainties.

we have strengthened
and reinforced the walls
around **our love garden.**

we know the weeds
that will choke and stifle
her growth,
we know the habits
that will kill
her fresh fruits
and infect her roots.

the flowers smell sweeter
in our garden, not because
we don't have weeds,
but because **we prune**
and care for them daily. ♥

r. A. bentinck

Happily Ever After

the happily ever after
we seek
is in our daily choices,

it's reinforced by
the actions we take,

it's in things
we focus on,

it's where we
channel our energies,

we must consciously create
our **mutual happiness**
daily. ♥

Picking Up The Pieces

it was only when
it all fell apart and
we started picking up
the pieces
that we saw the value
in what we had.

we swallowed humility
and reassembled
the broken pieces.

sometimes it takes
falling apart to see
the value in the pieces
we were too willing
to **throw away.** 🩶

r. A. bentinck

Fear

i was once schooled
by an elder who changed
my concept of love when
he posited,

*"you are either in love
or you are not"*

he assured me that
**genuine love,
knows no fear.**

*"love doesn't complicate things,
it is our fear of losing love,
and being hurt by love
that make things
unnecessarily complex."*
let's learn simplicity
by just **loving**
without setting restrictive
terms and conditions
that rob love
of **her true potential.** ♥

Valentine Poetry

Termites To Love

if you continue to assume
that anytime i'm
gone for too long
i'm **sneaking around.**

it doesn't do any good
to the **love foundation**
we are working so **hard**
to build.

if i have to unlock
my phone every time you have
doubts and fears

just to appease you
and keep the peace
it erodes the core of
the **trust** we are developing.

if you secretly explore
my wallet and
investigate my pockets
for evidence of infidelity

what signals are you
sending me about
the level of your trust
in me?

your assumptions are dangerous
they are termite to
our relationship. 🖤

r. A. bentinck

Contemplation

i'm sitting here with
so much weight
on my mind,

and i'm beginning
to wonder...

are we part of
each other's history?
or
are we part of
each other's destiny?

things and time
will be
the great revealer. 🖤

Valentine Poetry

Chapter Fourteen: Lasting Love

r. A. bentinck

Why

why are we still
together
after all
these **years?**

we give
each other
valuable reasons
to stay
daily.

there is no
magic formula,
or secret serum,
just daily love,
daily respect,
daily commitment,
daily trust,
daily discipline,
daily communication,
daily support.

every day
we make a commitment
to do everything
that strengthens
our relationship anew. 🩶

r. A. bentinck

Learners

we have learnt
to hold onto
each other
and
the sweetness
that
the present brings,

and we have learnt
to **let go**
of our **forgettable past**
and all its
bitterness. ♥

Adjustments

we have mastered
the art of fanning
the flickers
into
a **flame.**

we have cut off
the fingers
that are swift
to point
every time
we **consider blaming.**

we have **muzzled**
the pessimistic voices
that roam
in our head
from time to time.

we have learnt
to appreciate
the **sunshine**
as much as the **raindrops.**
we have lasted
this long
because we have
learnt the art
of **adjusting**
to the **changing times**
and **situations.** 🖤

r. A. bentinck

Daily Deposits

no, we don't have
the **perfect relationship**
and we both know that.

but, **what we do**
is make daily deposits
into what we have.

if we want more love,
we deposit more love
into what we share.

if we want more romance,
we infuse more romance
into our relationship account.
we give more unselfishly,
we take more time to support
and **complement each other.**

we never withdraw
more than we deposit
and we never ask for more than
we can give.
we make
daily deposits
into
our relationship account. ♥

Valentine Poetry

Daily Habits

every morning
**we make doing
the things that bring
a smile**
to our face
a habit
just as routine
as brushing our teeth.

at noontime
we make time
to nourish each other
with all the nutrients
that strengthens
our love bones
and muscles.
in the evening
we recap and celebrate
our daily gains
despite how small they might be,

and we never fall asleep
with bitterness
on the tips of our tongues
or at the center of
our hearts. ♥

r. A. bentinck

Damn!

damn,
the two of you still
together?

yeah,
that the kind
of **love we built together,**
it's the kind of love
**we continue
to foster.**

we will continue
to shock and **surprise
them.**

our love is private
not public,
our love clothed
in mutual support
and respect
not social media
glitch and glamour.
**what you fake in public
we live in private.**
our highlight reel
is for real. ♥

Valentine Poetry

Longevity

by the time
we found each other
we both would have been
bruised and battered
by the love
that **never lasted.**

but
we made an unspoken
commitment
to make what we
found in each other
last.

we survive the fires
of life,
we have lived
above low level
criticisms,
we have developed the art of
trust and transparency

they have all brought us
this far
and we intend to
keep growing and developing
a stronger love
every day. ♥

r. A. bentinck

Mastery

we are life long students
of this thing,
they call
love.

we are constantly
working
on
mastering
the art of
verbal
and
nonverbal
appreciation. 🖤

Valentine Poetry

No Retreat, No Surrender

when the tough time
came along
we stayed in the fight.

we cheerlead each other
when we were **winning**
and we became
cornerman and coach
when the battle was
bruising.

we could have given up
so many times
but we didn't.

we thought about
running away
but we stayed,
we contemplated
throwing in
the towel
but we stood
and fought through
every challenging round
we faced in life.

now we are here
celebrating
the sweetness of victory. ♥

r. A. bentinck

Revenge

we have made it
this far
not because
i never faltered or sinned.

i did.
many times before,

but she has never
reheat my failings
and **served them**
to me cold
with breakfast. ♥

Valentine Poetry

Story Time

once upon a time,
there was a man
who met a woman

and
he fell in love with
her smile,

the sparkle in
her eyes,

and the way
she made him feel.

them,
he promised himself
that he will make it
his daily duty
to do things
that will **brighten**
her smile,

add more sparkles
to her eyes
and
make him feel the way
he did
the first time they met,
every day. 🖤

r. A. bentinck

Time, Love And Tenderness

time.
we know we don't
own it
so we take time to **flow**
with it.

love.
we know its
not a fairytale
so we take time
to build the storybook love
we seek.

tenderness.
we know it's an important
component
to everything we share

and we keep
it's level of importance
at the **pinnacle**
of all that we do
and share. ♥

Without a Word

we don't need
to repeat it **daily.**

our committed actions
overtime
has built
a firm foundation
against
the shifting tides
and gale winds.

we don't need
to say it,
we can feel it
in **our synced vibes,**

we can see it
from the look
in each other's eyes.
we don't have to say
the words,
love is felt daily. ♥

r. A. bentinck

The Little Things

she is skilled
at finding ways
to make me
laugh a little harder,

while minimizing
my sadness.

she pours
so much happiness
into **our relationship**
giving tons of reasons

to smile a whole lot more. ♥

About The Author

r. A. Bentinck is the author of several poetry collections, including his debut book, *Of all the Lilies, Underneath the Poetry with My Girl, Underneath the Poetry and Bad Girl Stricken, Underneath the Poetry with Her Diary, Seduced, Sultry, The Flaws in Our Teen and Falling for Petals*.

Some of his books have also been translated in several foreign languages including, French, Spanish and Latin.

Bentinck is an Educator and an Artist who is focusing at this time on his self-publishing business while tutoring part-time at the E.R. Burrowes School of Art as a painting and drawing Tutor.

Bentinck is a graduate of the University of Guyana with a B. A. Degree in Fine Arts (Hons) and a Diploma in Education (Administration).

r. A. bentinck

www.ingramcontent.com/pod-product-compliance
Lightning Source LLC
Chambersburg PA
CBHW031948070426
42453CB00006BA/140